Popular Culture:
1960–1979

Michael Burgan

Raintree

www.raintreepublishers.co.uk
Visit our website to find out
more information about
Raintree books.

To order:
☏ Phone 0845 6044371
🖹 Fax +44 (0) 1865 312263
🖳 Email myorders@raintreepublishers.co.uk

Customers from outside the UK please telephone +44 1865 312262

Raintree is an imprint of Capstone Global Library
Limited, a company incorporated in England and Wales
having its registered office at 7 Pilgrim Street, London,
EC4V 6LB – Registered company number: 6695582

Text © Capstone Global Library Limited 2013
First published in hardback in 2013
The moral rights of the proprietor have been asserted.

Edited by Adam Miller, Andrew Farrow, and
  Adrian Vigliano
Designed by Richard Parker
Original illustrations © Capstone Global Ltd 2013
Illustrations by Richard Parker
Picture research by Mica Brancic
Originated by Capstone Global Library Ltd
Printed and bound in China by Leo Paper Products Ltd

ISBN 978 1 406 24023 8
16 15 14 13 12
10 9 8 7 6 5 4 3 2 1

British Library Cataloguing in Publication Data
TO COME
A full catalogue record for this book is available from
the British Library.

Acknowledgements
We would like to thank the following for permission
to reproduce photographs: Alamy p. 12 (© Lebrecht
Music and Arts Photo Library/Philip Grey); Corbis
pp. 15 (© Hulton-Deutsch Collection), 21 (Sygma/©
Michael Norcia), 25 (© Michael Ochs Archives), 27, 53
(© Bettmann); Getty Images pp. 5, 17, 20 (Michael Ochs
Archives), 6 (Redferns/Jan Persson), 7 (Lee Lockwood//
Time Life Pictures), 9 ("National Archives/Handout"),
11 (Ron Howard/Redferns), 13 (GAB Archive/
Redferns), 14 (Hulton Archive/Keystone), 19 (Richard
E. Aaron/Redferns), 18 (Hulton Archive/Michael
Putland), 23 (Popperfoto), 26 (Virginia Turbett/
Redferns), 29 ("Moviepix"), 33 (CBS Photo Archive),
37 (Hulton Archive/Alan Howard), 41 (Hulton
Archive/Apic), 45 (Time Life Pictures/Bill Pierce), 50
(CBS Photo Archive), 35 (Hulton Archive/Archive
Photos), 49 (Gamma-Keystone/Keystone-France);
The Kobal Collection p. 43 (United Artists); NASA p.
39; Photoshot p. 32 (© Starstock/Lucas Films); Press
Association Images p. 42 (AP); Rex Features pp. 30, 46
(Everett Collection). Background images and design
features reproduced with permission of Shutterstock.

Cover photograph of a couple disco dancing reproduced
with the permission of Getty Images (Hulton Archive/©
Dennis Hallinan).

Every effort has been made to contact copyright holders
of any material reproduced in this book. Any omissions
will be rectified in subsequent printings if notice is
given to the publisher.

Contents

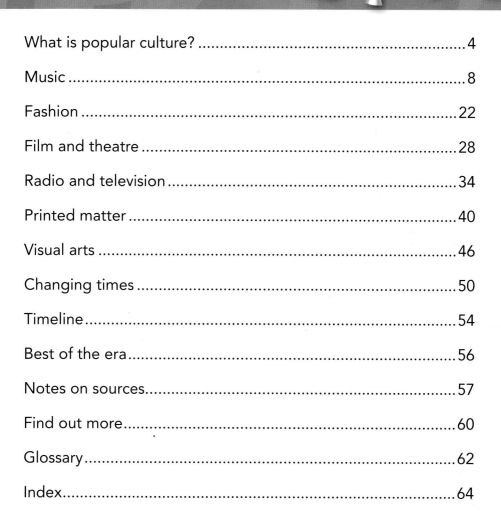

Some words are printed in bold, **like this**. You can find out what they mean by looking in the glossary.

What is popular culture?

If you've ever read a comic book, worn the latest fashion, or listened to the radio, you know something about pop culture. Pop – short for "popular" – culture surrounds us every day. The adverts you see, the TV shows and films you watch, the video games you play – these are part of pop culture, too.

Something becomes part of pop culture when it's experienced by many people almost at once, such as the latest YouTube video. Long before the internet, other forms of technology played a key role in creating pop culture. Starting in the 1920s, radio and films were key transmitters of pop culture. Everyone in a country could easily listen to the same songs and watch the same films. During the 1950s, television became another major force in pop culture. For the first time, millions of people could see arts, entertainment, and news in their own homes while others experienced the same thing. During the 1960s and 1970s, television continued to play a huge role in shaping pop culture. So did older media, such as radio, newspapers, and magazines.

Pop culture is not always about technology. Wearing certain clothes, such as blue jeans or T-shirts, can be an expression of pop culture. So can a simple image, such as the yellow smiley face of the 1970s, which is still seen today.

Teen culture

The pop culture of the 1960s continued a trend started the decade before: the influence of the young. During World War II (1939–1945), the demands of war kept many young adults from marrying and starting families. Afterwards, couples finally had a chance to have children, and the United Kingdom, the United States, and other nations saw a large rise in their birth rates. This population explosion was called the baby boom. The people born between 1946 and the early 1960s are often called baby boomers.[1]

Colour TV

Starting in the late 1940s, several US companies began to consider colour television broadcasting. Although some shows were shown in colour during the 1950s, colour television did not become widespread in the United States and Europe until the late 1960s and 1970s. Thanks to **satellites** sending TV signals thousands of kilometres, in 1967 British viewers saw their first live, colour coverage of a US sporting event – a golf match.[2]

The British rock band the Animals performs on the American 1960s TV show *Hullabaloo*. Bands of the era also performed on the British show *Top of the Pops*.

CULTURE IN CONTEXT

The artist Andy Warhol helped shape pop culture during the 1960s and 1970s. In 1968 he said, "In the future everyone will be world-famous for 15 minutes."[3] For most people, 15 minutes of fame is still not a reality. Warhol, though, realized how quickly ideas spread in pop culture – and then, just as often, quickly fade away.

A rising economy

In Europe, the years after World War II saw a slow economic recovery from the war's destruction. The United States, however, was luckier, as it had mostly escaped direct attack. Billions of dollars of US aid helped Europe rebuild, while millions of Americans went to college and bought new homes.[4]

By the late 1950s, many of the baby boomers had money to spend on consumer goods, leisure, and entertainment, thanks to their parents. Companies began targeting products and services at the boomers. Rock and roll records and films with teen stars were just two examples of this. The desire to appeal to teens kept rising during the 1960s, with adverts featuring toys, games, and foods for kids.

The threat of war

The era, though, had a darker side. At the end of World War II, the United States, the United Kingdom, and their democratic **allies** confronted **communist** nations led by the Soviet Union. The tension between the two sides was called the **Cold War**. Many people feared a **nuclear** war. Each side had thousands of nuclear missiles that could wipe out entire cities with almost no notice. Pop culture of the 1960s and 1970s sometimes explored the Cold War conflict and the fears it created.

Pete Townshend of the band the Who wrote the popular song "My Generation", which praised young people and made fun of the elderly. It included the line, "Hope I die before I get old".

The Cold War also led to real wars in parts of the world. The United States and Australia were just two countries that tried to prevent a communist takeover of South Vietnam. Many young Americans opposed the Vietnam War (1959–1975), leading to large protests. Many young men also opposed the draft, which would force them to fight in a war they believed was wrong. Young people across the **Western** world had a growing sense that their leaders did not always do what was right.

The Cold War and the desire for change among the young affected pop culture. Musicians sang against the Vietnam War. Many young people wore clothes and hairstyles their parents disliked, to show they rejected the older generation's **values**. These youths were often called hippies, and they had their own distinct pop culture. Young people in general seemed to seek greater freedom, and in the United Kingdom the 1960s were sometimes called the Swinging Sixties.

The face of the communist rebel Che Guevera often appeared on posters and T-shirts popular with Western youth as a form of protest against parents and leaders.

A different decade

Even before the Vietnam War was over, the great era of protests ended. Hippie clothing and protest songs were replaced with more glamorous styles and disco music. The 1970s were labelled the "Me Decade", as the young – and not-so-young – seemed more focused than ever on their own needs. But women, blacks, gays, and others still worked for change. Their efforts became part of the pop culture, too.

Music

Music seemed to fill the air during the 1960s. Small, battery-powered radios let people carry tunes wherever they went. So did portable record players. Bands sometimes played outside in parks, and many TV programmes featured the music of the day's most popular groups.

Music was one of the most influential aspects of pop culture. It entertained, provided the rhythm for new dances, and sometimes featured words that called for great social change. Four main styles of music defined the era, with musicians from one **genre** sometimes borrowing from another. The spread of music through radio and TV quickly exposed everyone to new ideas. All the music had some roots in even earlier styles. The pop music of the 1960s was an exciting blend of the old and the new.

Protest songs

During the 1950s, African Americans began calling for equal treatment under the law—their **civil rights**. That drive gathered steam in the 1960s, as blacks and whites marched together, protesting against **segregation** and violence towards blacks. The protesters often sang a new version of an old song heard in African American churches, "We Shall Overcome".[1] Other protest songs came out of the folk music tradition of the South, which had spread across America during the 1930s. Woody Guthrie helped create this kind of protest music. Playing just an acoustic guitar, he sang about the struggles of the poor in a rich country. Often, he put his words to old folk songs.

CULTURE IN CONTEXT

Young people in communist nations enjoyed music from the United States and Western Europe – when they could hear it. Communist leaders disliked Western culture in general and feared the influence of music that might make people question the government. Simply playing Western-style rock music was a form of protest – and dangerous. The Czech band Plastic People of the Universe, formed in 1968, was often denied permission to play publicly and was once arrested. It had to play secret concerts to avoid arrest.[2]

Joan Baez and Bob Dylan sometimes performed together, and she often sang his songs.

Dylan, Baez, and others

During the 1950s, Pete Seeger continued the Guthrie style, performing in a group and on his own. Seeger and Guthrie then influenced the first famous 1960s protest singers. These included Joan Baez and Bob Dylan. Baez was active in the civil rights movement, and she insisted that blacks and whites be allowed to sit together at her concerts. In 1962, she was featured on the cover of *Time*, a major American weekly magazine.[3]

Like Guthrie, Dylan sometimes put his words to old tunes. Dylan protested the treatment of blacks and the horrors of war. In 1963, he seemed to sum up the thoughts of many people, as he sang "the times they are a-changin'". The 1960s would not be like other decades before it. Dylan also sang that the answer to important questions was "blowin' in the wind". The pop culture he was helping to shape seemed to be part of that "wind".

9

A new kind of rhythm and blues

Protest music of the 1960s reflected a continuation of past musical styles. So did the changing sounds coming from African American recording artists. The blues had been born in the South, created by the children and grandchildren of former slaves. It then spread north and westward as African Americans sought work across the country. By the 1940s, rhythm and blues (R&B) described music with blues roots, but with added brass – usually saxophones – and electric instruments.[4] R&B continued to change during the 1950s, and finally combined elements of the blues and **gospel** with rock and popular music. Two cities, Detroit and Memphis, became famous for recording studios that featured a distinct African American sound.

The Motown sound

In Detroit, Michigan, Motown was the product of Berry Gordy, a songwriter who began recording various black singers. Some of the company's biggest stars were Smokey Robinson and the Miracles, the Temptations, Marvin Gaye, and Diana Ross and the Supremes. A later hit group was the Jackson 5, which featured a 10-year-old Michael Jackson.[5] The best Motown songs were usually danceable and upbeat, and appealed to both white and black audiences. It was, as the company said, "the sound of young America" – and beyond.[6]

By the early 1970s, Marvin Gaye had joined rock and folk singers in addressing social issues. The 1971 hit "Mercy Mercy Me" looked at environmental concerns – air pollution, overcrowding, the poisoning of fish. In "What's Going On", Gaye spoke out against war and violence of all kinds.

Stax

Another record company, Stax, created the Memphis sound. This R&B relied on brass instruments and the organ sound of Booker T. Jones, who performed on many Stax hits. His own group, Booker T. and the MG's, recorded the popular instrumental "Green Onions". Other hits by Stax artists included "In the Midnight Hour" by Wilson Pickett and "(Sitting on) The Dock of the Bay" by Otis Redding. Although she didn't record for Stax, Aretha Franklin worked with Memphis musicians.[7] Her soulful singing of Redding's "Respect" and other songs made her a star.

Stevie Wonder (1950-)

In 1963, Motown released a single by a blind, 12-year-old-musician called "Little" Stevie Wonder. The song, "Fingertips, Part 2", reached number one on the **record charts**. Wonder later dropped "Little" from his name, but he continued to create hit records. While Motown tightly controlled what most of its artists recorded, by the early 1970s Wonder had complete freedom over his music. He also played most of the instruments on his records. Wonder's music ranged from slow love songs to hard-driving tunes, and like other artists of the era, he sometimes wrote about social and political issues. "Living for the City", for example, dealt with the dangers of growing up on crime-ridden city streets. Wonder continued to record and perform into the twenty-first century.[8]

From Jamaica, with soul

Hundreds of years ago, the British took African slaves to the Caribbean island of Jamaica. The slaves were eventually freed, and Jamaica won its independence in 1962. Through the centuries, the Africans there blended their own musical traditions with European music. By the 1950s, American R&B and soul music was part of this mix, because Jamaicans could hear them on the radio. These forms influenced a Jamaican musical style known as ska. The new musical form was even more rhythmic and danceable than R&B, with a distinct Jamaican way of stressing certain beats.[9] Over time ska led to reggae. It had the same distinctive beat, but it was played at a slower pace. Reggae also featured bass and drums rather than the horns used in ska. The music was sometimes called Jamaican soul, reflecting the influence of soul music, another name for the Memphis sound and music that combined gospel and R&B.[10]

Jamaican music of all kinds made its way to the United Kingdom, where thousands of black Jamaicans had settled. During the 1960s, many white British youths danced to ska in discos.[11] By the end of the 1960s, music fans in both Europe and North America could hear reggae on the radio. Soon, white recording artists were also using the reggae style.[12]

The Specials started a revival of ska music in the UK in the late 1970s. This photo shows them performing live in London in 1979.

Bob Marley recorded his first song in 1962 and helped form the Wailers the following year.

Bob Marley and the Wailers

By the early 1970s, Bob Marley and Wailers emerged as reggae's top group. Marley wrote songs that became hits for others. The famous guitarist Eric Clapton, for example, recorded Marley's "I Shot the Sheriff". Marley and his band also had their own hits, such as "No Woman, No Cry" and "Get Up, Stand Up". The latter song, like much of the music of the 1960s and early 1970s, dealt with political concerns. Marley told his listeners to stand up for their rights and "don't give up the fight" for equality. Marley died in 1981, at the age of just 36, from cancer.[13] His influence, though, remained strong in reggae, which is still played today. In 1999, the US magazine *Time* named his *Exodus* (1977) the greatest album of the twentieth century.[14] Several of his children also became reggae artists.

Quote

"Bob Marley ... was the man who introduced the world to the mystic power of reggae. He was a true rocker at heart, and as a songwriter, he brought the lyrical force of Bob Dylan, the personal charisma of John Lennon, and the essential vocal stylings of Smokey Robinson into one voice."[15]

Jann Wenner, founder of *Rolling Stone* magazine

The British Invasion

The influence of American music, both black and white, reached far beyond the Caribbean. Starting in the 1950s, rock and roll was played around the world. Rock drew on such black musical styles as the blues and R&B, and the country and bluegrass music favoured by whites. The youth of the United Kingdom who grew up listening to rock began recording their own blues-based music during the early 1960s. Beginning with the Beatles, a number of British groups began releasing hit songs in the United States and then toured that country and other parts of the world. The Beatles led what was called the British Invasion.

The Beatles

John, Paul, George, and Ringo – millions of music fans knew the Beatles by just their first names. They began playing songs by American blues and rock groups, then Paul McCartney and John Lennon began to write their own songs, with pleasant melodies and words about young love. By 1963, the Beatles had their first number one records in the United Kingdom, and "Beatlemania" began. Screaming fans – mostly girls – came to their concerts, and some chased the band after the shows.[16] The mania hit the United States the next year, when the band performed live on TV on the popular *Ed Sullivan Show*. Soon the band was also appearing on products such as toys and masks, and shops even began selling Beatles wigs.

The Beatles prepare to leave London in 1965 to perform in the United States. Along with making music, the band appeared in several films.

Mick Jagger (front) and Keith Richards (far right) were the main songwriters of the Rolling Stones, who recorded into the twenty-first century.

A changing "invasion"

Other British bands soon followed the Beatles in becoming stars both at home and abroad. The best included the Kinks, the Who, the Animals, the Yardbirds, and the Rolling Stones. Some, such as the Stones, stuck closer to the roots of American blues.[17] The best also changed their sound as they grew older. By 1966, with the album *Revolver*, the Beatles were writing more complex words and experimenting with different kinds of music.

Playing with tape

During the 1960s, music was recorded on magnetic tape. For the song "Tomorrow Never Knows" the Beatles took musical notes and the sound of common items, such as a ticking clock, and recorded them over and over at different speeds. These "tape loops" helped give the song a foreign, strange sound.[18] Other musicians also made their own loops, and the sound became a key factor in what became known as psychedelic music (see page 16).

Music hard and soft

The Beatles, like other young people of the 1960s, experimented with illegal drugs. Marijuana and more powerful chemicals could alter their users' sense of time and distort what the users saw and heard. The drug LSD in particular created this so-called "psychedelic" effect.[19] A number of rock bands created music that either tried to recreate the feelings of a psychedelic drug experience or enhance the distorted sense of sound the drugs created.

In the United States, much of the psychedelic movement was centred around San Francisco, home of the Grateful Dead. The band often played on drugs, and a single song could stretch on for 15 or 20 minutes.[20] San Francisco was associated with "hippies" and the **counterculture** they represented. These young people rejected traditional values by wearing long hair, doing drugs, and listening to music. Some protested against the Vietnam War. Others wanted to spread a message of love. Other musicians tied to the hippies included Jefferson Airplane, the Doors, and Jimi Hendrix.[21] In the United Kingdom, Pink Floyd was the most influential psychedelic band. Its greatest hit of the era was *Dark Side of the Moon*. Released in 1973, it became a huge international seller.

"Pirate" radio

During the 1960s, the British government tightly controlled radio in the United Kingdom. Young people could not always hear the most exciting, new music. In 1964, a ship anchored off the coast of England began broadcasting the music not heard on the BBC. This floating station was called Radio Caroline and was known as pirate radio. Later that year it was joined by Radio London and several other pirate stations that played the latest in rock and R&B for British youth. The British government shut down the pirates in 1967, though Radio Caroline remained on the air until the next year.[22]

CULTURE IN CONTEXT

The 1960s saw the first outdoor rock concerts, or festivals, that went on for several days. The first large festival lasted for three days in Monterey, California, in 1967.[23] Woodstock, held in New York in 1969, was the most famous. About 400,000 people attended that three-day event. The show was promoted as "three days of peace and music" and became the symbol of the hippie movement.[24] Unfortunately, later that year a murder marred another festival, held at Altamont, California, but music festivals continued through the 1970s and are still popular today.

Another side of music

Not everyone in the1960s took drugs or listened to rock music, however. Welsh singer Tom Jones had a number of hit songs and a successful TV show popular with a wide range of women. "Bubblegum" music had bouncy tunes and simple lyrics aimed at children and young teens. One example was "Yummy, Yummy, Yummy (I Got Love in My Tummy)" by the Ohio Express.[25] However, the music preferred by the older baby boomers truly defined the music of the era.

This colourful 1967 poster of Bob Dylan had a psychedelic look. It was included with Dylan's first album of greatest hits.

New styles in the 1970s

In 1970, the Beatles split up, though individually the four musicians continued to record music. The same year, the popular blues-rock singer Janis Joplin died after taking too much of the drug heroin. Within a year, both Jimi Hendrix and Jim Morrison of the Doors had also died. They had been drug users and, like Joplin, often drank heavily. The deaths seemed to show the downside of the hippie era.

With the new decade, new styles of rock music emerged. Already, in 1969, Led Zeppelin helped to create heavy metal, also sometimes called hard rock. This music was still based in the blues, but songs were often fast and played at high volumes. Black Sabbath and Kiss were other popular heavy metal bands of the 1970s.

Glam rock

Glam, or glitter, rock presented another approach to music. Glam bands often wore fancy, even strange outfits and make-up. They also appeared **androgynous** – men dressed like women and often wore make-up. In the United Kingdom, Marc Bolan of the group T. Rex was the first big star of glam rock.[26] He was followed by David Bowie (pictured right), Slade, and Sweet. In the United States, Lou Reed, for a time, and the band the New York Dolls sported the androgynous look tied to glitter rock.[27]

David Bowie (1947-)

The cover of David Bowie's album *Aladdin Sane* (1973) shows him with orange hair and colourful make-up all over his body. The image was a prime example of the shocking look many glam bands sought. Bowie was also an excellent songwriter and performer. He had a background in art and could play several instruments, including the saxophone. Bowie influenced other musicians with both his songs and his flair for costumes and dramatic live concerts.

Punk

By the mid-1970s, many of the popular bands from the 1960s were still recording, but some teens wanted something new. In both the United States and the United Kingdom, the punk movement began. An early influence in the United States was the Ramones. Dressed in blue jeans and dark glasses, they played short, fast songs at high volume. The UK band the Sex Pistols appeared soon after the Ramones. They were managed by Malcolm McLaren. He gave the Pistols their name in 1975 and renamed the lead singer Johnny Rotten.[28] The anger in their music reflected the lives of much of British youth, who faced a bad **economy**.[29] One Pistols song said Britain had "no future".[30] The Clash soon followed the Pistols, and was a more talented punk band that played other musical styles, including reggae (see page 12).

Quote

"The popularity of punk rock was, in effect, due to the fact that it made ugliness beautiful."[31]

Malcolm McLaren

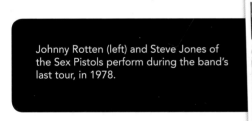

Johnny Rotten (left) and Steve Jones of the Sex Pistols perform during the band's last tour, in 1978.

In the United States, the early punk scene was centred in New York City. The New York Dolls, despite their glam image, played music with the energy of punk.[32] Starting around 1975, the nightclub CBGB featured the Ramones. Other bands that played there did not play the same style of songs, but they were associated with the city's punk scene. These groups included the Talking Heads, Patti Smith, Television, and Blondie.[33]

The fast pace and high energy of punk affected fans in different ways. Fights sometimes broke out at Sex Pistols shows. The band members added to the chaos by spitting from the stage.[34] Fans slam danced – throwing themselves into each other as they danced together. Even punk fashions reflected the movement's anger and disgust with "normal" society (see page 26).

On the dance floor

Another major musical movement began in the years of glam and just before the rise of punk. Disco, as it was called, had a very different sound. Its roots were in the danceable rhythms of R&B and the funk music of James Brown, the "godfather of soul". Its name came from *discotheque*. For years, discos had played recorded music where people could dance, often as part of a group, rather than with a partner. During the 1960s, discos had made new dances popular, such as the twist.[35]

By the 1970s, discos and the music they played were popular with black and gay audiences. For gay men, private clubs with recorded music offered them an important social gathering place. The **disc jockeys** (DJs) who played the music often became well known, as they carefully chose music that would keep dancers on the floor.[36] New York's Paradise Garage was perhaps the most influential of the gay dance clubs. Extended sets of dance music appeared later at many other clubs.[37]

This still of John Travolta from the movie *Saturday Night Fever* was one of the best-known images of the disco era.

A wider appeal

By the mid-1970s, disco music spread into the larger culture. Even people who didn't go to clubs could hear disco hits on the radio. Some of the top artists were Donna Summer, KC and the Sunshine Band, and Kool and the Gang. In 1977, the movie *Saturday Night Fever* produced several hit songs sung by the British group the Bee Gees. It was about a white disco dancer from Brooklyn, played by a young John Travolta.

The Village People also had several disco hits. The group was started by two French songwriters and featured several singers dressed in various costumes, including a cowboy, a construction worker, and a sailor. The group's lyrics looked at gay culture – one of the first times pop music openly addressed this topic.[38] The Village People's biggest hit, "YMCA", is still popular today.

Dancers at New York's Studio 54, one of the most famous discos of the late 1970s.

Did you know?

Disco was not liked by some rock fans, who were mostly white. A "disco demolition" night to blow up records brought in by fans was held during a Chicago White Sox game. Some members of the crowd ran on to the field after the explosion. Critics of the event saw the anti-disco feelings as racist and **homophobic**, since many fans of disco were African American or gay.[39]

Fashion

Every era has distinct clothing, jewellery, and hairstyles that together are known as fashion. During the 1960s, designers tried to appeal to young people by introducing new styles and materials not used before. The fashions of the 1960s and 1970s were often linked to the world of music. As musicians wore certain styles, their fans copied them.

Going "mod"

A major fashion movement called mod came out of Swinging London and its new focus on youth. Mod, short for "modern", referred to clothes that featured bold colours and geometric designs. Men's clothing also got fancier, with bright shirts and boots with slightly high heels.

UK designer Mary Quant helped start the mod trend, selling her clothes from a shop on King's Road in London. By the middle of the 1960s, that area and nearby Carnaby Street were the centre of mod fashion. The clothes spread beyond London and the United Kingdom as British bands helped draw the world's attention to the fashions of their homeland.

Quant helped make popular one of the most **radical** pieces of clothing of the era: the miniskirt. The bottom of a miniskirt came up six inches or more above a woman's knee. The skirt offended some people who did not think women should show so much of their legs. The miniskirt was part of a new, casual attitude towards the body and sex that many older people disliked.[1]

Other people associated with mod London styles were Vidal Sassoon, a hair stylist, and designer John Bates. Sassoon created short styles cut with severe angles and lines. Bates helped make the miniskirt popular, and he designed clothes for both famous stars and the mass public who shopped in department stores.

While the miniskirt exposed a woman's upper legs, tall plastic boots often covered up the lower part. French designer André Courrèges created go-go boots in 1964 for his models. They were meant to be fashion, not outerwear to keep feet dry. Soon women were wearing them on the dance floor, too, paired with their miniskirts.[2]

Did you know?

The Austin Mini Cooper, a tiny British car and the model for today's Mini Cooper, supposedly inspired Mary Quant to make miniskirts.[3]

Long and tall

The 1970s saw a reaction to the miniskirt. Designers went to the other extreme with the maxi skirt, which reached to the floor. In between the maxi and the mini was the midi, which usually fell to a woman's upper calf.[4]

As skirts got long, some shoes got very tall. Both the glam rock movement and disco inspired "platform shoes", boots, and shoes with heels several inches high. The shoes were considered **unisex**, meaning both men and women wore this fashion, which was meant to be fun for the wearer and shocking to the average person.[5]

Twiggy

To model their new clothes, fashion designers often seek tall, thin women. One of the slimmest ever was Twiggy (shown above in 1966), who became famous modelling mod fashions. Her real name was Lesley Hornby, and in 1966 a new short haircut helped frame her pretty face. She soon appeared in many fashion magazines, becoming one of the world's first **supermodels**. Her thin body and short hair gave her an androgynous look that would spread among men and women in the years to come. Twiggy's success went beyond modelling. She became a pop star, recorded a song, and appeared on TV shows. The US toy company Mattel even released a Twiggy version of the Barbie doll. Another company sold large, false eyelashes like the ones she wore.[6]

Fashion from the music world

As with their music, the Beatles also had an influence on fashion. They began their career wearing the black leather jackets popular during the 1950s. By the time Beatlemania hit, they were wearing mod-style suits.[7]

What struck most people, especially adults, about the Beatles was their hair. They wore it long compared to most men of the time, based on a haircut they first got while playing in Germany.[8] Soon the style was called a Beatles haircut, though it reminded some people of a mop, leading to another name for the cut: mop top (see the Beatles photo on page 14). Longer, straight hair became popular with young men, and the length continued to grow during the decade. Some African American men and women also grew their hair long, creating a round hairstyle called an Afro.

The Beatles drew on different sources for their clothes. By 1966, George Harrison was interested in Indian culture and music, and he and the band spent time in India. The bright clothes they wore for the album *Sgt. Pepper's Lonely Hearts Club Band* were partly inspired by the vivid colours of some traditional Indian clothing.[9] The band members also helped popularize the Nehru jacket. This was an Indian-style jacket with a short collar that stands up around the neck.

Hippie clothing

The outfits from *Sgt. Pepper's Lonely Hearts Club Band* were also part of the psychedelic era.[10] Young people who embraced hippie culture often favoured bright colours and wild patterns. Some began to make their own clothing, by dyeing T-shirts and making beaded headbands. For women, long, flowing peasant dresses and skirts were popular. Other female hippies wore short shirts and halter tops, which exposed the stomach. For men, waistcoats with **fringes** often went over T-shirts. Both men and women sometimes wore peace symbol jewellery.

Young people seeking a hippie look sometimes bought used clothing or old army shirts. The style allowed people to dress almost any way they wanted. The hippie fashion was not as stylish as the mod clothes favoured by many in the United Kingdom, though the hippie look became popular in many parts of the world.

Hippie fashion featured a wide range of clothing, from hats to beads. Jeans were common for both men and women. This photo shows the American band Jefferson Airplane in concert in 1967, wearing a variety of hippie fashions.

Tie-dyeing

Sometimes technology can be simple, as in turning a plain shirt into a burst of colour. Many young people of the 1960s used kits containing dye to create tie-dyed fashions. The "tie" referred to using rubber bands or string to tie off sections of the shirt or other items of clothing. The shirt was then dipped into buckets of dye, each with a different colour. The tying of the fabric created colourful patterns, which were revealed when the bands or string were removed.[11]

The punk look

Punk music of the 1970s had its own fashion movement, too. In this case, the clothes came before the music. In 1971, designer Vivienne Westwood opened a clothes shop with Malcolm McLaren in London. They sold leather clothing that drew on popular styles of the 1950s, then added zippers and chains to some items. The store had several names before the pair called it Sex.[12] Some of the look for the clothing came from styles McLaren saw while visiting New York. The punk rocker Richard Hell had ripped up his clothes, and McLaren copied the look. Hell also designed a T-shirt that said, "Please kill me", and McLaren later sold shirts with other outrageous slogans. The influence of Hell's band the Neon Boys (later renamed Television, after Hell left the band) and the New York Dolls also led McLaren to form the Sex Pistols.[13]

Punk haircuts were distinct as well. Some punks wore their hair in long spikes, held up by hair gel. Others wore Mohawks, with the sides of their heads shaved and a tall strip of hair in the centre.

These teen punks wear leather jackets with metal studs, a common part of punk fashion.

Disco fashions

If punk was about rebellion and offending, the disco scene offered a very different approach to fashion. For some dancers, their goal was to impress others with their taste in clothes. The fabrics, such as lycra, were meant to stretch while dancing, and help reflect the lights that constantly swirled over the dance floor. In the early years of disco, some women wore hot pants – extremely small shorts that drew attention to their legs. Off the dance floor, more women began wearing trousers or trouser suits, with matching tops and slacks. For men, a common look on the dance floor was a suit jacket over a shirt that was unbuttoned at the chest.[14] The actor John Travolta made this look popular in the film *Saturday Night Fever* (see page 20).[15] The lightweight suits worn to discos and parties were called leisure suits, to make the distinction between them and formal suits worn for work.

As always, jeans

During the 1960s and 1970s, jeans were worn by teens, adults, musicians, artists – almost everyone seemed to favour jeans. While blue jeans were most common, white jeans were a fad during the 1960s. Hippies and punks favoured old jeans, often ripped or patched. Some jeans came with their leg

bottoms flared out, a look called bell-bottoms. Some young people added cheap jewellery or **embroidery** to their denim to give it a distinct look.[16] With the disco craze, some designers introduced expensive jeans meant for the dance floor. Studio 54, a popular New York disco, even sold its own brand of these "designer jeans".[17]

Denim, the material used to make blue jeans, was also used to make jackets, and during the early 1970s, one car-maker used denim to cover some car seats.

Film and theatre

In the early 1960s, old film genres, or styles, still remained popular. Parents took children to such musicals as *Mary Poppins* and *The Sound of Music*. The adults enjoyed traditional films by such actors as Cary Grant and Katharine Hepburn, who had been stars since the 1930s. Movies also began to explore the growing, more open expression of sex and questioning of rules. Violence and swearing also appeared on screen like never before. Films were becoming more like real life, which meant they might be shocking or have a tragic ending.

Some important films of the 1960s

In the 1960s, a number of films that were produced in the United States reflected the attitudes of the era. *The Graduate* (1967) explored the story of a bored young man who ends up in a relationship with an older, married woman. The film featured music by Simon and Garfunkel, and several of the songs are still popular today. *Easy Rider* (1969) focused on motorcycle-riding hippies taking a road trip across America and choosing to live differently from average Americans. *Bonnie and Clyde* (1967) made two real-life criminals seem sexy and fun. The violence in that film and in the western *The Wild Bunch* (1969) was more realistic than in earlier films. Even more gruesome was *Night of the Living Dead* (1968), a horror film that showed zombies eating people. It helped inspire zombie movies as a new genre within horror. The 1960s also saw the first films in the popular series about the handsome British spy James Bond, 007. Bond used high-tech gadgets to track down criminals who represented the communists the West were fighting during the Cold War. He also found time to date many beautiful women.[1]

Science fiction

Science fiction films were not new, but they entered the psychedelic era with *2001: A Space Odyssey* (1968). The film appeared the year before humans first landed on the moon. For part of the film, an astronaut – and the viewers – experience colourful lights and images similar to the ones some rock musicians used on stage. Several Japanese science fiction films of the era reflected the fears of nuclear **radiation**. The first of these films, including *Godzilla*, appeared during the 1950s, but Godzilla and other giant creatures appeared in new Japanese films throughout the 1960s.

Faye Dunaway starred as Bonnie Parker, one of the famous criminals featured in the film *Bonnie and Clyde*.

European influence

The 1966 film *Blow Up* was set in London, showing the world of mod fashion in Swinging London (see page 22). Its director, however, was an Italian, and films shot across Europe became influential in the United States and the United Kingdom. Some of these European artists focused on the inner lives of their characters, trying to use images to show their thoughts and feelings.[3] French directors shaped a movement called New Wave, which became popular in the late 1950s and continued into the 1960s. The filmmakers used natural sets and lighting, moving outside the large studios often used in Hollywood and London. They also moved quickly from scene to scene or between images in the same scene.[4]

New directions

The 1970s saw a new generation of filmmakers appear in Hollywood, the centre of the film industry. Some were early baby boomers, some were a little older. These directors had more power over shaping their films than many earlier directors did.[5] They continued to push the limits on how much sex and violence could appear on screen. The best were superb storytellers as well, and focused on the darker side of human life.

Francis Ford Coppola showed his skills in *The Godfather* (1972) and its 1974 **sequel** *The Godfather, Part II*. These films focused on the violent world of an Italian American crime family, and suggested that running such a family was just another form of business. The films boosted the careers of two new stars, Robert De Niro and Al Pacino. The two actors were not considered to be as handsome as the traditional Hollywood stars. They relied on talent as much as looks to impress audiences.

Horror and science fiction of a different kind

Steven Spielberg made several films in the early 1970s, but *Jaws* (1975) was the one that made him well known around the world. The film focuses on three men trying to kill a deadly shark. Spielberg used three different mechanical sharks to portray the killer shark on screen. He would go on to make other films that relied on special effects, such as the science fiction movie *Close Encounters of the Third Kind* (1977).

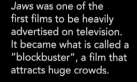

Jaws was one of the first films to be heavily advertised on television. It became what is called a "blockbuster", a film that attracts huge crowds.

The true king of film science fiction was George Lucas. His film *Star Wars* (1977) became the first of six films set in a distant part of space. The film led to many popular dolls and toys based on the movie's characters and settings.[6] *Star Wars* also made a star of Harrison Ford, who became an action hero in the later *Indiana Jones* films by Spielberg.

A look at the past

The United States military left Vietnam in 1973, but the war there remained a key cultural issue for some Americans. Several films that examined the war's effects on soldiers and their families soon followed. De Niro starred in one of them, *The Deer Hunter* (1978). Coppola released *Apocalypse Now* (1978), which suggested that the war – and any war – could drive people crazy. *Coming Home* (1978) dealt with the return of one disabled soldier. It featured Jane Fonda, one of the top female actors of the 1970s. Years earlier, she had angered many Americans when she visited North Vietnam, the main US enemy during the war.

One popular film of the 1970s did not seem to fit the new style. It did not challenge common values. Instead, it focused on a simple man following his dream to be the best boxer he could be. *Rocky* was the first of six movies about this character, played by Sylvester Stallone. He also wrote the film, which won the 1976 Academy Award for Best Picture.

Year	Best Picture	Best Director
1970	*Patton*	Franklin J. Schaffner (*Patton*)
1971	*The French Connection*	William Friedkin (*The French Connection*)
1972	*The Godfather*	Bob Fosse (*Cabaret*)
1973	*The Sting*	George Roy Hill (*The Sting*)
1974	*The Godfather, Part II*	Francis Ford Coppola (*The Godfather, Part II*)
1975	*One Flew Over the Cuckoo's Nest*	Milos Forman (*One Flew Over the Cuckoo's Nest*)
1976	*Rocky*	John G. Avildsen (*Rocky*)
1977	*Annie Hall*	Woody Allen (*Annie Hall*)
1978	*The Deer Hunter*	Michael Cimino (*The Deer Hunter*)
1979	*Kramer vs. Kramer*	Robert Benton (*Kramer vs. Kramer*)

A list of the Academy Award Best Picture and Best Director recipients of the 1970s. Most of these movies are still popular with film viewers today.

Rise of new genres

Horror, already a broad film genre, saw the rise of a specific type of horror film: the slasher movie. These films centre around a killer who chases down and murders a number of victims, often teens. *Psycho* has been called an early slasher film, and a few other 1960s films had elements of this genre. The 1974 film *The Texas Chainsaw Massacre* had more of the extreme violence associated with the slasher films that gained popularity during the 1980s.[7]

Another genre popular in the 1970s was disaster movies. In these films, large numbers of people faced death because of either a natural disaster or some sort of technical failure. Some of these included *Airport* (1970), about a plane with a bomber on board, and *The Poseidon Adventure* (1972), about a ship overturned by a giant wave. *The Towering Inferno* (1974) was set in a burning skyscraper. The films created tension as audiences wondered who would live and who would die in the face of the disaster.

Special effects

Disaster movies and other genres of the era relied on special effects to convince audiences that what they saw was real. At times that meant using models of large buildings and then destroying them on film, as in *Earthquake* (1974).[8]

Detailed models were also used for some of the spacecraft in *Star Wars*. However, that film was most famous for using computers to control the movement of cameras. This was the first time this method was used for a major film. *Star Wars* was also an early example of a movie composed of computer-generated images (CGI), which are used today in many films.[9]

In *Star Wars*, special effects made a model of the Death Star, a giant spaceship, look real.

Leonard Nimoy as Mr Spock (left) and William Shatner as Captain Kirk were the stars of the TV show *Star Trek*. They also played these characters in several films.

Theatre

Theatre did not have the same impact on pop culture of this era as films and music did. Fewer people could access the theatres that staged major works than could go to the local cinema or hear songs on the radio. Still, several plays did reflect cultural trends of the time. The musical *Hair* (1967) focused on the rise of the hippie movement. Several songs from the show became hits on the radio. The same was true with *Jesus Christ Superstar* (1971). This musical is about the last days of Jesus. Both were called "rock musicals", because they brought rock music to the theatre for the first time.[10]

Both also had critics of their content. *Hair* shocked some people by showing nudity on stage, while *Superstar* challenged religious belief and suggested Jesus was just a man, and not the son of God, as Christians believe.[11] Less controversial was *Grease* (1971), which looked back to the pop culture of the 1950s, especially the music.[12] At the same time, though, it dealt with themes that had become common during the 1960s, such as challenging authority. A 1978 film version was also a huge hit.[13]

Radio and television

Music was an essential part of 1960s and 1970s pop culture, and television and radio were major sources of it. Several shows on either side of the Atlantic focused on new music. In the United Kingdom, John Peel left pirate radio to work for the British Broadcasting Corporation. His "Peel Sessions" started in 1967. Peel played recordings of bands performing live just for the show. He was also famous for discovering new bands and playing musical styles before they became widely popular, such as reggae and punk. Peel's show continued into the early twenty-first century, until his death in 2004.[1]

FM radio was also becoming popular. FM stations provided better sound than the more common AM. Many FM stations also gave disc jockeys greater freedom to play what whey wanted. By the 1970s, FM stations tended to focus on just one style of music per station, such as oldies.[2] In the United Kingdom, **commercial** radio stations appeared for the first time during the early 1970s, broadcasting on both FM and medium wave.[3]

AM Versus FM

Amplitude modulation (AM) signals can travel great distances but until recently, AM stations could not broadcast in stereo. **Frequency modulation (FM)** signals cannot travel as far, but even in the 1960s FM stations could broadcast in stereo and without as much static as AM.[4]

Changes on TV

On TV, pop music appeared in different forms. Variety shows such as *The Ed Sullivan Show* featured new, popular bands. The Beatles got their own show – as cartoon characters. One musical group, the Monkees, was created by a TV network so the band could have its own show and also record music.[5]

TV was more than just a source of music. Many programmes reflected larger concerns of the 1960s. Cold War spying was the subject of such shows as *The Man From U.N.C.L.E.* and *I Spy*. *The Prisoner* was a UK show about a former spy, "Number 6", imprisoned in an isolated seaside village. *Get Smart* was a **sitcom** that made fun of spy shows and films. Science fiction also appeared in several forms. *Star Trek* was first shown in 1966, with characters from several ethnic backgrounds. The first of many *Star Trek* films appeared during the 1970s. Science fiction was also aimed at children. A British puppet show called *Thunderbirds* featured a variety of spacecraft flown by the Tracy family.[6]

CULTURE IN CONTEXT

The interest in science fiction on television was strong in Japan, and some of the shows were eventually shown in other countries. The Japanese had a cartoon called *Astro Boy*, which featured a heroic robot boy.[7] *Ultraman* used actors to tell the story of an alien who comes to Earth to help humans fight monsters. First aired in 1966, different versions of *Ultraman* were broadcast in Japan for 40 years. US versions of the show were also produced.[8] Robots and monsters were both part of a series called *Johnny Sokko and His Flying Robot*, which first appeared in 1967.[9]

Actors and puppets pose on the set of the television show *Sesame Street* in 1969.

CULTURE IN CONTEXT

By the end of the baby boom, some people thought television could be a good way to teach young children the basics of numbers and letters. *Sesame Street* was introduced in 1969 to do this in a fun way. Songs and comedy scenes with puppets called the Muppets combined entertainment and education. *Sesame Street* helped the Muppets become stars on their own, and they later had their own evening TV show and several films.[10]

For teens and adults, television offered a wide range of programmes. Some of the most popular were situation comedies – "sitcoms" for short. These shows usually focused on a small group of people in one setting, such as a home or workplace. Some event or situation, such as a family crisis, triggers the story in each **episode**, and the characters must respond to it.

Popular sitcoms

A British programme called *Till Death Us Do Part* helped change the range of sitcoms. The show first appeared in 1965 and addressed racial, social, and political issues from the point of view of a working-class family. The show also highlighted the generation gap between the generally **conservative** father and his more **liberal** daughter and son-in-law.[11] The series ran for several years and inspired a similar show in the United States called *All in the Family*. The US version tackled such issues as the Vietnam War and racism, and led to other sitcoms that dealt with important topics in the United States.

In the United States, other popular sitcoms of the 1970s included *The Mary Tyler Moore Show* and *M*A*S*H*. In the first, Mary Tyler Moore played a character named Mary Richards, and the show focused on the life of a single, working woman. In part, the show reflected the rise of **feminism** during the 1960s and 1970s, which called for greater equality for women in the home and workplace.[12] *M*A*S*H* was set in an army hospital during the Korean War of the 1950s. Its views reflected some of the anti-war feelings stirred by the Vietnam War. Unlike most sitcoms, it often dealt openly with serious issues such as death and suffering.[13]

Video games

In 1975, TV viewers seeking a new kind of fun turned to *Pong*. It was the first successful video game in arcades, and that year a home version was introduced. Two players bounced a small white square back and forth across the screen, in a video version of Ping-Pong. Within two years, gamers could buy systems that let them play different games on the same machine, using separate cartridges. Though the first home video game systems had very little computer memory compared to today's games,[14] they were the beginning of the video-game craze that continues today, with people playing on home computers and phones as well as televisions.

Other TV comedies

By the 1960s, television already had a history of successful comedy shows based on short scenes called sketches. New shows, however, introduced new comic forms. For two years at the end of the decade, *Laugh-In* was the most popular show in the United States. Instead of longer sketches it had very short scenes and jokes that were told rapidly, moving quickly from one to the next. Phrases used on the show were repeated across the country, such as "Sock it to me, baby", and "Verrry interrrresting".[15]

Around the same time, a group of British comics created *Monty Python's Flying Circus* for the BBC. At times they did more traditional sketches, but some scenes blended into others or ended without warning. Mixed in were animated scenes with **surreal** images. The show was later aired in the United States, and Monty Python made several popular films during the 1970s and 1980s.

One of the longest-running US TV shows ever was a sketch-comedy show launched in 1975. *Saturday Night Live* aired late at night and allowed its comedians to deal with such topics as sex and drugs. Over the years, a number of the show's stars went on to become successful film stars, including John Belushi and Bill Murray.

In one sketch from their TV show, the members of Monty Python make fun of a popular British news reporter.

The changing face of TV

Viewers also turned to TV for serious stories. During the day, US **soap operas** drew large audiences. These programmes told the continuing stories of large numbers of people, often focusing on their love lives and personal problems.[16] US night-time soaps began in 1978 with *Dallas*. During the 1980s it became a major hit around the world and led to other night-time soaps, such as *Dynasty* and *Knot's Landing*.[17] In the United Kingdom, soap operas were shown in the early evening, and the most popular was *Coronation Street*.

Dallas was first broadcast as a miniseries before becoming an ongoing programmes. The miniseries genre began in the United Kingdom, with programmes that told long, complicated stories over several episodes. The series were designed to have a set number of episodes, as opposed to running as long as the programme stayed popular. Some of the UK shows became popular in the United States, and US producers began making their own miniseries during the 1970s. The most popular of these was *Roots*, based on a book by the African American writer Alex Haley. The story focused on the history of slavery in America and its impact on one black family. *Roots* became the most-watched show of the decade and helped educate Americans about a part of US history not usually seen on TV. The show was also popular around the world.[18]

In the early 1960s, a US official called television a "vast wasteland".[19] He meant that too many programmes did not offer viewers anything positive, such as knowledge about the world. However, programmes such as *Roots* showed the power of TV to educate – even though some critics thought at times it was too much like a soap opera.[20] TV could also unite people, as they watched live sporting or news events as they happened.

The VCR

TV stations had recorded programmes on magnetic tape since the 1950s. Starting in 1969, small plastic cases called cassettes held videotape that could be used to record programmes as they were broadcast. Videocassette recorders (VCRs) let people record shows and watch them when they wanted. Later, films could be bought on tape to watch at home. The success of VCRs led to better devices for recording television at home, such as today's digital video recorders.

Tragedy and triumphs

In 1963, US television viewers were shocked to see the murder of Lee Harvey Oswald. A Texas nightclub owner named Jack Ruby shot him on live television. Just days before, Oswald had been arrested for the assassination of President John F. Kennedy. The news of that event was aired on TV, and the stations showed no entertainment for almost four days. Everything focused on the shooting and the president's funeral, which was watched on more than 40 million US TV sets and broadcast in other countries as well.[21]

Television also brought the Vietnam War into people's homes. It was the first war that was televised.[22] When a popular and widely respected newscaster named Walter Cronkite suggested that the United States could not win this war, President Lyndon B. Johnson worried that he would continue to lose support for the already unpopular war.[23]

Thanks to satellites, the whole world could learn about important events at the same time. Another painful event was the kidnapping and killing of Israeli athletes by Arab terrorists. This tragedy occurred during the 1972 Summer Olympics in Munich, Germany. Television also showed historic moments, such as the first humans walking on the Moon. Hundreds of millions of people around the world saw this 1969 event.[24]

Images of Neil Armstrong, the first human to step on the Moon, and Buzz Aldrin (shown here) were broadcast over about 238,000 miles, the average distance between Earth and the Moon.

Did you know?

In the early 2000s, the US space agency NASA found old videos of the live broadcast of the 1969 moonwalk. It used computers to improve the quality of the video and released it to the public in 2009, giving the best view yet of that historic moment.[25]

Printed matter

Television was the newest **medium** for spreading pop culture, but older forms still had a role to play during the 1960s and 1970s. Books and magazines often reflected the many changes of the era.

Fiction of the 1960s

Catch-22 (1961) by Joseph Heller was a popular novel set during World War II. However, the issues it raised were current, as it made fun of dealing with government and business officials who control many parts of life. The book's title entered the language as a term for an impossible or senseless problem that can never be solved. Ken Kesey's *One Flew Over the Cuckoo's Nest* (1962) showed a similar struggle as its main character challenged the power of the head nurse in a hospital for the mentally ill. Kurt Vonnegut published several popular books, including *Slaughterhouse-Five* (1969). Also set during World War II, it reflected the anti-war mood that was growing at the time.

Kingsley Amis was a major writer in the United Kingdom. He had started his career in the 1950s with comic novels, but during the 1960s wrote in several genres. These included science fiction and horror. He continued to write until the early 1990s. One of his best books, *Take a Girl Like You* (1960), seemed to offer a view of the **permissive** sexual values that would become more common as the decade went on.

Margaret Drabble was a British author who explored the role of women in society. Her well-received books included *The Millstone* (1965) and *Jerusalem the Golden* (1967), as well as other works written in later decades.

The lighter side

Not all the writings of the 1960s were so serious. Spy stories were as popular in novels as they were on screen when they were adapted for films. British author John le Carré was one of the best in the spy genre. His first great work was *The Spy Who Came in From the Cold* (1963). Others that followed included *Tinker, Tailor, Soldier, Spy* (1974) and *Smiley's People* (1979).

For children, popular books included the rhyming books of the American, Theodor Geisel, known as Dr. Seuss. He wrote *Green Eggs and Ham* in 1960, and his early books have remained popular up to today. So has the work of Roald Dahl. His *Charlie and the Chocolate Factory* (1964) and *James and the Giant Peach* (1961) are still read today. Another popular form of printed

material for children was the comic book. During the 1960s, Marvel Comics introduced several new characters that are still part of pop culture in books and on film. They included Iron Man and Spider-Man.

Science fiction and fantasy

Two old genres got a boost during the 1960s and 1970s. Science fiction had its own "New Wave", as younger science fiction writers of the era turned away from the space travel and detailed science of earlier writers. They wanted to explore human relationships and social issues of the day. Some of the masters of the New Wave included Philip K. Dick and Ursula K. Le Guin. Dick's *Do Androids Dream of Electric Sheep?* (1968) was the basis for a later film, *Blade Runner* (1982). Le Guin's *The Left Hand of Darkness* (1969) explored the roles men and women play in society. She also created her own fictional world, Earthsea, and wrote a number of books with that setting. The first, *The Wizard of Earthsea*, appeared in 1968.

Thanks to the bite from a radioactive spider, Peter Parker has the power to turn into the superhero Spider-Man.

A world of hobbits

J. R. R. Tolkien created perhaps the most famous fictional world ever, Middle Earth. His books about the hobbits and other beings that live there were first released during the 1930s (*The Hobbit*) and 1950s (*The Lord of the Rings*). However, it was during the 1960s that Tolkien's books truly entered pop culture, as many baby boomers discovered them for the first time, thanks to new paperback editions. The themes of battling evil, powerful forces, and saving the natural world appealed to members of the counterculture.

Non-fiction

Non-fiction books of the era addressed many of the important issues of the day. In 1963, Betty Friedan helped open a new chapter in the feminist movement (often called "second-wave feminism") with her book *The Feminine Mystique*. In it Friedan argued that modern Western society did not let women develop their full talents as individuals. Eldridge Cleaver set down his views on racism while exploring his own life in *Soul on Ice* (1968). His ideas were at the base of the Black Power movement, which called on African Americans to rely on themselves, not white society, to improve their lives.

Several journalists wrote articles and books that explored the changing times in a personal way. At times their actions and ideas became part of the story, as well as the events they covered. The top names in this "New Journalism" included Hunter S. Thompson and Tom Wolfe. Drugs were often a theme of these books. Thompson wrote about his own drug use while covering politics and sports. Wolfe made Ken Kesey and his group the Merry Pranksters famous in *The Electric Kool-Aid Acid Test* (1968).

American journalist and political activist Gloria Steinem cofounded the feminist-themed magazine *Ms.* in 1972.

Newspapers and magazines

The changing times of the era led to new magazines and newspapers. With the rise of feminism and an effort to give women more political power, Gloria Steinem cofounded *Ms.* in 1972. The magazine explored the roles women played and how their rights and views were sometimes denied by men. Even earlier, underground papers and magazines arose. They were meant to be alternatives to the papers put out by large companies and dealt with issues young people cared about. In the United Kingdom, *International Times* and *Friends* were two popular underground papers. Many Americans read *Rolling Stone*. The magazine was started to provide music news, but it also published New Journalism writers and covered US politics. Both *Rolling Stone* and *Ms.* are still published today, reflecting the importance of the issues they address.

Fiction of the 1970s

The hippie movement died down during the 1970s, but many readers still looked to the counterculture for new ideas. The interest in Eastern religions remained strong and helped shape the **New Age** approach to spirituality. One novel offered a suggestion for building happier, more meaningful lives. *Jonathan Livingston Seagull* (1970), by Richard Bach, told the life of a seagull that pursues his own path to happiness. The book was a fable meant to give humans hope that they could do the same.

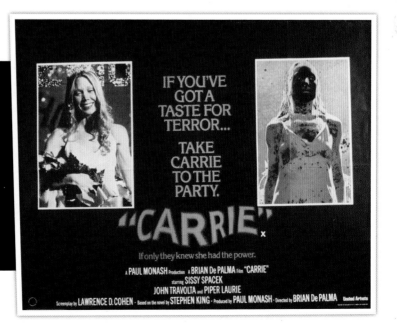

Famous horror writer Stephen King had his first success with his book *Carrie* (1974). The main character uses special powers to get back at fellow students who make fun of her. This poster is from the book's film adaptation in 1976.

The book quickly sold more than one million copies. A more serious, and still popular, writer to emerge during the 1970s was Toni Morrison. Her *Song of Solomon* (1977) deals with African American folktales and the traditional art of telling stories.

In genre fiction, horror fans enjoyed William Peter Blatty's *The Exorcist* (1971), which was also made into a popular movie. Stephen King had his first success, publishing such books as *Carrie* (1974) and *The Shining* (1977). These and other King books were also made into films. In the United Kingdom, former politician Jeffrey Archer wrote several books at the end of the decade, dealing with politics and business. His *Kane and Abel* (1979) became one of the best-selling novels of all time.

Important non-fiction

The 1960s saw the beginning of the modern environmental movement. Governments began passing laws that tried to reduce pollution, and more people became interested in ways they could reduce the damage they did to the environment.

The *Whole Earth Catalog* was part of this early "green" movement. It first appeared in 1968 and was published once a year for the next several years. By 1971, it was selling hundreds of thousands of copies around the world. Random issues of the publication appeared throughout the 1970s. Articles ranged from how to gather wild mushrooms to exploring the connection of all living things on the planet.

Self-help books were also popular during the 1970s and have remained popular to this day. The genre offered readers ways to improve their lives, from losing weight to building better relationships. One bestseller of the decade was *I'm OK, You're OK* by Thomas Harris. It was published in 1969 but became a bestseller during the 1970s.

The book helped readers better understand themselves and their relationships with others.

Quote

"*The Whole Earth Catalog* ... was one of the bibles of my generation ... It was sort of like Google in paperback form, 35 years before Google came along."
Steve Jobs, co-founder of Apple

The Watergate scandal, which led to President Richard Nixon lying to the public and then resigning from office, was the subject of the popular non-fiction book *All the President's Men* (1974).

CULTURE IN CONTEXT

The Watergate scandal and the resignation of President Richard Nixon dominated US politics during the early 1970s. In the best-selling *All the President's Men* (1974), reporters Bob Woodward and Carl Bernstein described how they uncovered the illegal activities of men connected to Nixon. Watergate was the name of a hotel and office building that Nixon's men broke into, hoping to spy on political rivals. Nixon tried to cover up what he knew about the crime and his link to the burglars. As the truth about the Watergate affair slowly came out, Nixon faced **impeachment** by the US Congress. Rather than be forced out of office, he resigned in August 1974 — two months after *All the President's Men* was published. The book led many Americans to question their government, as they learned they had been lied to about key events.

Visual arts

In the 1960s, fine arts and pop culture began to blend in the field of visual arts. An art movement called **pop art** began in the 1950s, but had its greatest impact during the 1960s.[1] The creators of pop art turned to items from everyday life as their subjects, from comic books to beer cans. At times it made fun of or illustrated the post-war culture that was obsessed with buying goods.[2]

Andy Warhol (centre) with the Velvet Underground, singer Nico (bottom left), and others who performed as part of the Exploding Plastic Inevitable. These performances blended different art forms, and were sometimes called "happenings".

Pop art

The British artist Richard Hamilton brought new meaning to the term *pop art* during the early 1960s. He had been one of the artists who had helped define the style in the previous decade.[3] In 1961, Roy Lichtenstein began creating some of the most recognizable images of early pop art. He took images from comic books and painted them on large canvases, often including words as well. To create the scenes he used different coloured dots, which became a distinctive part of his style.[4]

Andy Warhol

During this time, Andy Warhol was painting comic book images. He had achieved fame in 1962 with a series of paintings of Campbell's Soup cans, each a different kind of soup.[5] Next he turned to sculpture, painting wooden boxes so they looked like the cardboard boxes used to hold common products, such as ketchup. His later paintings included portraits of famous people, such as the film star Marilyn Monroe. The success of Warhol's art made him a pop-culture star himself, a role he embraced throughout the 1970s and beyond.[6] Some of Warhol's works now sell for millions of dollars.[7]

CULTURE IN CONTEXT

In 1964, Andy Warhol opened a space in New York where he created new art. Called the Factory, the space – even in the bathroom – was covered with silver paint and foil.[8] It was the scene of parties as well as work. At the Factory, Warhol also made films, though they were not designed for commercial cinemas. They were silent and shot in black-and-white. Some went on for hours, with no story. One showed his friend sleeping. Warhol also worked with the Velvet Underground, a rock band. Warhol promoted a stage show with the band called the Exploding Plastic Inevitable. Bright, coloured lights filled the stage as the musicians played and friends of Warhol danced. The artist's films were also shown.[9] This mixture of different art forms in one performance was part of the art and music worlds of the era.

Pop art and beyond

Even before Andy Warhol's rise to fame, Claes Oldenburg was creating his own kind of pop art sculpture. He used canvas and vinyl to make soft models of common items, such as a toilet and a piece of cake.[10] At times the sculptures were much larger than the real-life subject. Into the 1970s, Oldenburg moved away from soft art to make giant outdoor sculptures, such as one of a 45-foot-tall clothespeg.[11]

In the United Kingdom, David Hockney made art that blended pop art with earlier styles of modern art.[12] Later in his career, he made photo collages.[13] A collage is a mixture of different images and art forms in one work. Richard Hamilton had done some in the early years of pop art, and other artists also used this form.

Everyday images

Visual art of the era also included images tied to products and advertising. One of the most famous images of modern times first appeared during the 1960s – the yellow smiley face. At the end of the decade, two brothers named Bernard and Murray Spain took their own version of the face and added the words "Have a happy day". The men put the image and the words on many common items, such as T-shirts, badges, and posters. The Spains thought people needed to see something positive after the Vietnam War and racial violence of the 1960s. Other companies saw how popular the smiley face was becoming and sold their goods with the image.[14]

During the 1970s, the Japanese company Sanrio created a cartoon kitten to use on products it hoped to sell to young girls. That was the birth of Hello Kitty, which remains popular today. The kitten has appeared on 15,000 different products since it first appeared. Earlier, Sanrio had placed images of strawberries on its products, and for a time it ran a shop called the Strawberry Shop in San Francisco. The company was started to satisfy a part of Japanese culture – the exchanging of small gifts between friends and relatives. Now its products are sold all over the world.[15]

Niki de Saint Phalle was a French artist who is often associated with pop art. Here she is posing with several of her Nana sculptures in 1964. The Nanas were sculptures that depicted female figures, often very large. The Nanas shocked some people, who thought they looked too wild, aggressive, and powerful. Others thought the sculptures addressed important issues related to women and society.

Changing times

People often think in terms of decades when looking back at history. The calendar seems to give a natural starting and stopping point. However, the cultural developments of the 1960s and 1970s can't always be so easily defined by time. The development of some ideas that shaped the hippie movement started with the Beats of the 1950s. Many of them lived in San Francisco, explored Eastern religion, and challenged the values of mainstream society.[1] Some parts of hippie dress and counterculture attitudes carried over into the 1970s, and can still be found today.

Era of peace and violence

The Beatles were one of the greatest pop culture influences of the 1960s. In 1967, they sang "All You Need Is Love". That song had a message many people wanted to share. Yet the decade was also marked by great violence, beginning with the shooting of President John F. Kennedy in 1963 and the Vietnam War. Even protests that started out peacefully, such as those against the war and for civil rights, sometimes turned violent.

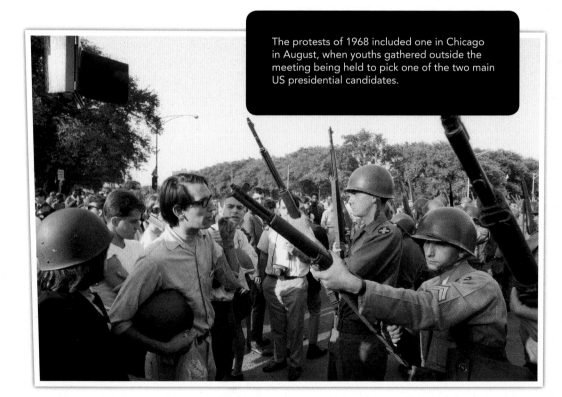

The protests of 1968 included one in Chicago in August, when youths gathered outside the meeting being held to pick one of the two main US presidential candidates.

The war led to protests and the questioning of governments' actions by many youths. Some protesters thought the Western world was merely trying to force its will on smaller, poorer countries. In the United States, some young men protested against a war they did not want to help fight. While the Vietnam War directly affected people in the West and on the battlefield, the wider Cold War created an atmosphere of fear. No one knew if the West and the communist nations would avoid a nuclear war, which could kill millions of people.

Another movement might have been even more important, as it had a longer-lasting effect. People previously denied full legal and social rights began, or continued, to demand equality. They included women, African Americans, Native Americans, Hispanics, and homosexuals. Amid these calls for change, which occasionally got angry or violent, the hippie movement stressed peace and love – and the use of drugs, which are now known to pose health dangers. Music, books, films, and other media reflected all these trends.

CULTURE IN CONTEXT

Each year is filled with memorable moments, but 1968 seemed to sum up much of the 1960s. In several countries, violence broke out between protesting youths and police. Some shared a sense that the war in Vietnam was wrong. More generally, they thought their generation had to challenge the older generations that ran society, and fix the problems the leaders had created. In 1968, youths protested in cities throughout the world, including Chicago, Paris, Mexico City, and London. In Prague, Czechoslovakia, the youth and others tried to challenge communist rule. Military troops crushed this rebellion. Riots in Paris lasted more than a week. Race also played a part in some US riots, as some blacks showed their anger over the killing of Martin Luther King Jr, the country's main civil rights leader. King had called for non-violent action, but many youths around the world were ready to fight. Most of the protests ended quickly, but they demonstrated a new willingness among many people to speak out loudly for change.[2]

Quote

"It was the first time ... the non-violent thing went right out the window ... police horses charging, people dragged through hedges and beaten up."[3]
Russell Hunter, observer of the London protest of 1968

Defining the 1970s

In some ways, the culture of the 1970s was a reaction to the extremes of the 1960s. Many people in the older generation grew tired of protests and sexual permissiveness. As early as 1964, Mary Whitehouse was trying to remove references to sex on British TV and preserve what she considered proper values. UK politician Margaret Thatcher supported her work.[4] In 1979, Thatcher was elected prime minister, and she promoted conservative values and free-market economic ideas in government and society. Ronald Reagan was elected US president the next year, and he shared those views – and a dislike of the youth rebellions of the 1960s.

Difficult times

Although the Vietnam War ended, the 1970s brought challenges that hit closer to home for many Westerners. Americans saw their president lie and give up his office. The British saw their economy decline, as many people lost their jobs in the middle of the decade. Job losses increased again as the 1980s began.[5] Many countries battled rising prices for petroleum products. Arab countries that produced much of that resource reduced their supply, as a protest against Western policies in the Middle East. Prices rose again in 1979, following a revolution in Iran, which was a major oil producer. The revolution put in place a strong anti-American government in Iran, which allowed students to kidnap dozens of Americans. To some Americans, the tumultuous political events of the 1970s, including the hostage crisis, the loss in Vietnam, and Watergate, displayed a weak America.

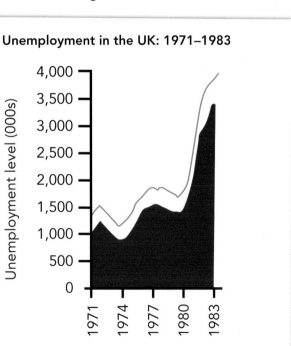

Unemployment in the UK: 1971–1983

This graph illustrates the declining economic situation people in the UK were dealing with during the 1970s and into the next decade.

Iranian students burn an American flag on top of the US embassy in Tehran, Iran, in 1979. Just days earlier the students had helped take over the embassy as well as a group of over 50 American hostages. The hostages were finally released over a year later, in 1981.

The pop culture of the 1970s reflected a growing sense of looking for pleasure while turning away from outer problems. American writer Tom Wolfe called the 1970s "the Me Decade". He and others attacked this sense of turning inward and seeking pleasure through sex, drugs, or buying goods. Another critic of the perceived selfishness was social critic Christopher Lasch. He said people were trying to use others for pleasure, rather than seeking it in themselves. The fascination with fame and celebrities was part of this, an idea Andy Warhol framed with his quote about 15 minutes of fame (see page 5). Yet even in the Me Decade, people could look beyond themselves. The call for equality among different groups went on. New causes, such as protecting the environment, won new supporters.

One word or idea cannot fully define any decade. The pop culture of the 1960s and 1970s reflected the interests and concerns of many people. Some music and other art were direct reflections of what was happening in the world. Others were creative expressions shaped by earlier art trends and ideas, and some was just pure entertainment. The best pop culture of the era still has influence today, helping to shape the pop culture of current times.

Timeline

1946
Beginning of the baby boom era

1950s
Civil rights movement grows in the United States

Writers called the Beats turn to Asia for spiritual insight

1962
Andy Warhol paints soup cans, an example of pop art

1963
The Beatles have their first number one song in the United Kingdom

Bob Dylan's song "The Times They Are a-Changin'" is released

Betty Friedan's *The Feminine Mystique* helps shape modern feminism

US President John F. Kennedy is killed

1964
"Beatlemania" goes to the United States

First pirate radio station appears off the coast of England

1965
The United States increases its involvement in the Vietnam War.

In the United Kingdom, *Till Death Us Do Part* first airs and influences other sitcoms with its look at the generation gap and other important cultural issues of the day

1966
Twiggy emerges as one of the top fashion models, and the miniskirt reflects the rise of "mod" clothing

Star Trek first appears on television

1967
Hair is the first successful rock musical

Monterey, California, is the site of the first major rock festival

Rolling Stone magazine is first published

Satellites send the first live, colour broadcast of a US sporting event to viewers in the United Kingdom

1968
In the middle of the rising feelings against the Vietnam War, John Wayne releases *The Green Berets*, a film that supports the war

1968 (continued)
Youths protest in various cities around the world, including Chicago, London, and Paris

African Americans riot in several cities after the killing of civil rights leader Martin Luther King Jr

1969
Led Zeppelin releases its first album and begins to shape heavy metal

People around the world watch the first Moon walk on TV

The Woodstock music festival draws 400,000 people

1971
Vivienne Westwood opens a clothing shop in London, selling what will become punk fashion

1972
The feminist magazine *Ms.* is first published

1973
US troops leave Vietnam

1974
Stephen King's first novel, *Carrie*, is published

The Watergate scandal forces Richard Nixon to resign as US president.

1975
Malcolm McLaren names the Sex Pistols

The *Pong* video game is introduced for home use

1977
The film *Saturday Night Fever* reflects the rise of disco in pop culture

George Lucas releases the first *Star Wars* film, which uses the most advanced special effects of the time

1978
Halloween is the first slasher film to reach a wide audience

1979
Margaret Thatcher becomes prime minister of the United Kingdom

US embassy in Tehran, Iran, is taken over by students and militants. Over 50 Americans are taken hostage.

Best of the era

The best way to find out about the pop culture of the 1960s and 1970s is to experience it for yourself. Here are some suggestions for the best or most typical examples that will give you a sense of the time:

Music

Are You Experienced (1967): Jimi Hendrix Experience
Highway 61 Revisited (1965): Bob Dylan
Innervisions (1973): Stevie Wonder
Led Zeppelin II (1969): Led Zeppelin
Live at the Apollo (1963): James Brown
My Generation (1965): The Who
Revolver (1966): The Beatles
The Rise and Fall of Ziggy Stardust (1972): David Bowie
Saturday Night Fever (1978): Original Soundtrack
What's Going On (1971): Marvin Gaye

Books

Franny and Zooey (1961): J. D. Salinger
The Spy Who Came in From the Cold (1964): John Le Carré
Curtain (1975): Agatha Christie
The Dead Zone (1979): Stephen King
Born Free (1960): Joy Adamson
Silent Spring (1962): Rachel Carson
In Cold Blood (1966): Truman Capote
All the President's Men (1974): Bob Woodward and Carl Bernstein
The Complete Book of Running (1978): James Fixx

Films

Films from the era with the most ticket sales worldwide since their original release (does not include rentals).

Film	Amount (US $)	Year released
Star Wars	797.9	1977
Grease	379.8	1978
The Exorcist	357.5	1973
Close Encounters of the Third Kind	300	1977
Superman	289.4	1978
The Godfather	244.9	1972
Saturday Night Fever	237.1	1977
Rocky	225	1976
101 Dalmatians	224	1961
Jaws 2	208.9	1978

Notes on sources

What is popular culture?

1. Dominic Sandbrook, "How the Baby Boomers Bust Britain," Mail Online, March 15, 2010, http://www.dailymail.co.uk/debate/article-1257631/How-baby-boomers-bust-Britain-Self-indulgence-left-country-financially-socially-morally-crippled.html.

2. Les Brown, *Encyclopedia of Television*, 3rd ed. (Canton, MI: Visible Ink Press, 1992), 122–23; British TV History, "Colour Television Chronology," http://www.tvhistory.btinternet.co.uk/html/colour_chronology.html.

3. Justin Kaplan, ed., *Bartlett's Familiar Quotations*, 16th ed. (Boston: Little, Brown and Company, 1992), 758.

4. Taylor Downing and Jeremy Isaacs, *Cold War: An Illustrated History 1945-1991* (Boston: Little, Brown and Company, 1992), 60.

Music

1. Ed Ward, "We Shall Overcome," Get Up Stand Up: The Power of Pop and Protest, http://www.pbs.org/wnet/getupstandup/music_overcome1.html.

2. Richie Unterberger, "The Plastic People of the Universe," http://www.richieunterberger.com/ppu.html.

3. "Chronology," Joan Baez.com, http://www.joanbaez.com/chronology.html.

4. Jim Miller, ed., *The Rolling Stone Illustrated History of Rock & Roll* (New York: Rolling Stone Press, 1976), 26.

5. Miller, *Illustrated History of Rock & Roll*, 230.

6. "Motown," Encyclopedia Britannica's Guide to Black History, http://www.britannica.com/blackhistory/article-9001781.

7. Miller, *Illustrated History of Rock & Roll*, 205.

8. Miller, *Illustrated History of Rock & Roll*, 338–39.

9. Simon Jones, *Black Culture, White Youth: Reggae Tradition From Jamaica to U.K.*, (London: Palgrave Macmillan, 1988), 19–23.

10. Miller, *Illustrated History of Rock & Roll*, 370; Stax Museum of American Soul Music, http://www.staxmuseum.com/.

11. Jones, *Black Culture, White Youth*, 87–88.

12. Miller, *Illustrated History of Rock & Roll*, 370

13. Jeffrey Brown, "30 Years After Bob Marley's Death," PBS NewsHour Art Beat, http://www.pbs.org/newshour/art/blog/2011/05/30-years-after-bob-marleys-death.html.

14. "The Best of the Century," *Time* Magazine, December 31, 1999, http://www.time.com/time/magazine/article/0,9171,993039-2,00.html.

15. "Bob Marley, Timeless and Universal," Wailers, http://wailers.com/news/articles/bob_marley_timeless_and_universal/

16. The Beatles, *The Beatles Anthology* (San Francisco: Chronicle Books, 2000), 92.

17. Miller, *Illustrated History of Rock & Roll*, 182.

18. The Beatles, *The Beatles Anthology*, 209-211.

19. John Philip Jenkins, "Psychedelic Drug," *Encyclopedia Britannica*, http://www.britannica.com/EBchecked/topic/481540/psychedelic-drug.

20. Miller, *Illustrated History of Rock & Roll*, 248.

21. Downing and Isaacs, *Cold War*, 254–55.

22. Mary Payne, "'It Was Time to Introduce American Top 40-Style Radio to the UK,'" Radio London, http://www.radiolondon.co.uk/kneesflashes/stationprofile/hist.html.

23. "Monterey Pop," Pennebaker Hegedus Films, http://www.phfilms.com/index.php/phf/film/the_monterey_pop_festival/.

24. Woodstock Festival History: August 15-16-17-18, 1969, Bethel Woods Center for the Arts, http://www.bethelwoodscenter.org/museum/festivalhistory.aspx.

25. David Mansour, *From Abba to Zoom: A Pop Culture Encyclopedia of the Late 20th Century* (Riverside, NJ: Andrews McMeel Publishing, 2005), 58.

26. "Biography for Marc Bolan," Internet Movie Database, http://www.imdb.com/name/nm0092647/bio.

27. Frank Hoffman and Robert Birkline, "Glitter Rock," Survey of American Popular Music, http://www.shsu.edu/~lis_fwh/book/hybrid_children_of_rock/Glitter%20Rock2.htm.

28. Gary Graff, "Malcolm McLaren, Former Sex Pistols Manager, Dies," *Billboard*, April 8, 2010, http://www.billboard.com/news/malcolm-mclaren-former-sex-pistols-manager-1004081674.story#/news/malcolm-mclaren-former-sex-pistols-manager-1004081674.story.

29. Iain Chambers, *Urban Rhythms: Pop Music and Popular Culture* (London: Palgrave MacMillan, 1986), 184.

30. "Sex Pistols Biography," *Rock and Roll Hall of Fame*, http://rockhall.com/inductees/sex-pistols/bio.

31. Murray Wardrop, "Malcolm McLaren: In His Own Words," *The Telegraph*, April 9, 2010, http://www.telegraph.co.uk/culture/music/music-news/7570928/Malcolm-McLaren-in-his-own-words.html.

32. "Proto-Punk," Allmusic, http://www.allmusic.com/explore/style/proto-punk-d2698.

33. "New York Punk," Allmusic, http://www.allmusic.com/explore/style/new-york-punk-d11367.

34. "Sex Pistols Biography," *Rock and Roll Hall of Fame*.

35. Hoffman and Birkline, "Disco Music," *Survey of American Popular Music*, http://www.shsu.edu/~lis_fwh/book/hybrid_children_of_rock/Disco2.htm.

36. Hoffman and Birkline, "Disco Music."

37. "Disco Pioneer Mel Cheren Dies at 74," Resident Advisor, December 12, 2007, http://www.residentadvisor.net/news.aspx?id=8995.

38. "Village People," Hollywood Star Walk, *Los Angeles Times*, http://projects.latimes.com/hollywood/star-walk/village-people/.

39. http://swindlemagazine.com/issue09/disco-demolition-night/.

Fashion

1. Sixties City, http://www.sixtiescity.com/Fashion/Fashion.shtm.

2. "Andres Courreges," Fashion Model Directory, http://www.fashionmodeldirectory.com/designers/andre-courreges/.

3. Harold Pace, "The Mini Evolution," Automedia.com, http://www.automedia.com/The_Mini_Evolution/res20040501me/1.

4. Susannah Conway, "The History of…the Maxi Skirt," *Independent*, October 18, 1998, http://www.independent.co.uk/life-style/the-history-of-the-maxi-skirt-down-to-the-ground-1179023.html.

5. Platform Shoes, http://www.platformshoe.org.

6. Twiggy, http://www.twiggylawson.co.uk/fashion.html#story.

7. Jahna Peloquin, "The Beatles and Fashion," Minnesota Public Radio, http://minnesota.publicradio.org/collections/special/columns/music_blog/archive/2009/09/meet_the_beatles_fashion.shtml.

8. The Beatles, *The Beatles Anthology*, 64.

9. Peloquin, "The Beatles and Fashion."

10. Adam Fox, "The Beatles: Style Icons," Ask Men, http://www.askmen.com/fashion/style_icon_60/82_the-beatles-style-icons.html.

11. "Tie-dyeing," Rit, http://www.ritdye.com/dyeing-techniques/tie-dyeing.

12. "430 Kings Road," Vivienne Westwood, http://www.viviennewestwood.co.uk/w/the-story/kings-road.

13. Sean O'Neal, "R.I.P. Malcolm McLaren," AV Club, April 8, 2010, http://www.avclub.com/articles/rip-malcolm-mclaren,39946/.

14. Pauline Weston Thomas, "The 70s Disco Fashion," Fashion-Era.com, http://www.fashion-era.com/1970s.htm.

15. "Saturday Night Fever: John Travolta's White Suit," Clothes on Film, http://clothesonfilm.com/saturday-night-fever-john-travolta-white-suit/3017/.

16. James Sullivan, *Jeans: A Cultural History of an American Icon* (New York: Gotham, 2006), 142.

17. Sullivan, *Jeans*, 149.

Film and theatre

1. Jeremy Black, "What We Can Learn from James Bond," History News Network, January 24, 2006, http://hnn.us/articles/3556.html.

2. "George Romero's *Night of the Living Dead*," Museum of Modern Art, http://www.moma.org/visit/calendar/films/565.

3. Alan Casty, *Development of the Film: An Interpretive History*, (New York: Harcourt Brace Jovanovich, 1973), 275.

4. David A. Cook, *A History of Narrative Film*, (New York: W. W. Norton & Company, 1981) 459–60.

5. Peter Biskind, *Easy Riders, Raging Bulls: How the Sex-Drugs-and-Rock 'N' Roll Generation Saved Hollywood* (New York: Simon and Schuster, 1998), 15.

6. Quentin Hardy, "The Force Is Strong in This One," *Forbes*, April 30, 2009, http://www.forbes.com/2009/04/30/star-wars-sanitswet-technology-personal-tech-star-wars_slide.html.

7. "Slasher Movies," Monster Movies, http://www.monsters-movies.com/slasher_movies.htm.

8. Tim Dirks, "Film Milestones in Visual and Special Effects," AMC Filmsite, http://www.filmsite.org/visualeffects9.html.

9. Tim Dirks, "CGI's Evolution From *Westworld* to *The Matrix* to *Sky Captain and the World of Tomorrow*," AMC Filmcritic.com, http://www.filmcritic.com/features/2009/05/cgi-movie-milestones.

10. James Rado, "Hairstory: The Story Behind the Story," Hair the Musical, February 14, 2009, http://www.hairthemusical.com/history.html.

11. "Some Things to Consider Before You Attend Jesus Christ Superstar," Free Presbyterian Church, http://www.freepres.org/pamphlet_details.asp?superstar.

12. Jim Jacobs, "The Glory of *Grease*," Grease the Musical, http://www.greasethemusical.co.uk/history.php.

13. Scott Miller, "*Inside Grease*," New Line Theater Grease, http://www.newlinetheatre.com/greasechapter.html.

Radio and television

1. "Legendary Radio DJ John Peel Dies," *BBC News*, October 26, 2004, http://news.bbc.co.uk/2/hi/entertainment/3955289.stm; Keeping It Peel, BBC, http://www.bbc.co.uk/radio1/johnpeel/sessions/.

2. Mike Adams, "A Century of Radio," California Radio Historical Society, http://www.californiahistoricalradio.com/100years.html.

3. "History of Radio Transmission Part 2: 1967 – Present," Frequency Finder UK, http://www.frequencyfinder.org.uk/trans_hist2.html.

4. "FM vs. AM: What's the Difference?" Radio Transmission, PBS, http://www.pbs.org/wgbh/aso/tryit/radio/radiorelayer.html.

5. Brown, *Encyclopedia of Television*, 360; Raj, "Rhino's Monkee History," March 30, 2011, The Monkees.net, http://www.monkees.net/rhinos-monkees-history.

6. Neal Midgley, "Gerry Anderson to Make New TV Series of Thunderbirds," *Telegraph*, January 11, 2011, http://www.telegraph.co.uk/culture/tvandradio/bbc/8253552/Gerry-Anderson-to-make-new-TV-series-of-Thunderbirds.html.

7. "Astroboy Manga Published in Shonen Magazine," Tezuka in English, http://tezukainenglish.com/?q=node/208.

8. Mark Schilling, "Ultraman...Forever!" *Japan Times*, November 12, 2006, http://search.japantimes.co.jp/cgi-bin/fl20061112x1.html

9. "*Johnny Sokko and His Flying Robot* Coming to MGM DVD on Demand," *Sci Fi Japan*, June 9, 2010, http://www.scifijapan.com/articles/2010/06/09/johnny-sokko-and-his-flying-robot-coming-to-mgm-dvd-on-demand/.

10. Brown, *Encyclopedia of Television*, 510–11.

11. "*Till Death Us Do Part*," The British Comedy Guide, http://www.comedy.co.uk/guide/tv/till_death_us_do_part/.

12. Ashley Hayes, *Dress, Dialogue, and Gender in the Mary Tyler Moore Show From 1970-1977*, http://etd.lsu.edu/docs/available/etd-11162010-004924/unrestricted/Hayes_Thesis.pdf.

13. Brown, *Encyclopedia of Television*, 341.

14. Jeff Tyson, "How Video Game Systems Work," How Stuff Works, http://www.howstuffworks.com/video-game2.htm.

15. Brown, *Encyclopedia of Television*, 470; "20 Most Popular TV Shows Each Year in the 1960's," Entertainment Scene, http://www.entertainmentscene.com/top_tv_shows_60s.html.

16. Brown, *Encyclopedia of Television*, 517.

17. Brown, *Encyclopedia of Television*, 144.

18. Roots, Warner TV, http://www.warnertv.com/shows/Roots?PHPSESSID=f953ea713c520e9f62adcf95a902dc7a; "Roots: U.S. Serial Drama," The Museum of Broadcast Communications, http://www.museum.tv/eotvsection.php?entrycode=roots.

19. Brown, *Encyclopedia of Television*, 357.

20. "Roots: U.S. Serial Drama," The Museum of Broadcast Communications.

21. "America's Long Vigil," History of American Broadcasting, http://jeff560.tripod.com/tvgjfk.html.

22. Harry G. Summers, *The Vietnam War Almanac* (New York: Presidio Press, 1999), 333.

23. Summers, *The Vietnam War Almanac*, 135.

24. Nell Greenfieldboyce, "Search Is on for Original Apollo 11 Footage," National Public Radio, July 31, 2006, http://www.npr.org/templates/story/story.php?storyId=5578853.

25. Greenfieldboyce, "Search Is on for Original Apollo 11 Footage."

Visual arts

1. Gardner's Art Through the Ages, 782–83.

2. "Career," The Warhol Museum, http://www.warhol.org/aboutandy/career.

3. Gardner's Art Through the Ages, 785.

4. Edward Lucie-Smith, "Roy Lichtenstein," The Artchive, http://www.artchive.com/artchive/L/lichtenstein.html.

5. "Andy Warhol Biography," The Warhol Museum, http://www.warhol.org/aboutandy/biography/.

6. "Career," The Warhol Museum.

7. Kelly Crow, "Bets in '11: Pop, Calder, Chinese Coins," *Wall Street Journal*, January 8, 2011, http://online.wsj.com/article/SB10001424052748704415104576065961534171834.html?mod=rss_Arts_and_Entertainment.

8. "Andy Warhol's Factory," Andywarholstars.org, http://www.warholstars.org/chron/factory63n7.html.

9. "Andy Warhol's Exploding Plastic Inevitable," The Experimental Films of John Behrens, http://www.jonbehrensfilms.com/experimental005.html.

10. Barbara Haskell, "Claes Oldenburg," The Museum of Modern Art, http://www.moma.org/collection/artist.php?artist_id=4397.

11. "PAFA Announces Claes Oldenburg Sculpture Commission for Plaza," Art Knowledge News, http://www.artknowledgenews.com/2010_07_10_00_07_14_pafa_announces_claes_oldenburg_sculpture_commission_for_plaza.html.

12. Arthur Marwick, *Culture in Britain Since 1945* (Oxford: Basil Blackwell, 1991), 110–12.

13. "About David Hockney," David Hockney.com, http://www.davidhockney.com/bio.shtml.

14. "Who Invented the Smiley Face?" Straight Dope, April 23, 1993, http://www.straightdope.com/columns/read/961/who-invented-the-smiley-face.

15. "Sanrio Company, Ltd.," Funding Universe, http://www.fundinguniverse.com/company-histories/Sanrio-Company-Ltd-Company-History.html.

Changing times

1. Edvin Beitiks, "The Beat Generation: Rebels, With Good Cause," *San Francisco Chronicle*, September 17, 1999, http://www.sfgate.com/cgi-bin/article.cgi?f=/e/a/1999/09/17/WEEKEND819.dtl.

2. Sean O'Hagen, "Everyone to the Barricades," *Observer*, January 20, 2008, http://www.guardian.co.uk/world/2008/jan/20/1968theyearofrevolt.features.

3. O'Hagen, "Everyone to the Barricades."

4. William Mees-Rogg, "Was Mary Whitehouse Right All Along?" *Times*, June 7, 2010, http://www.timesonline.co.uk/tol/comment/columnists/william_rees_mogg/article7145128.ece.

5. Marwick, *Culture in Britain Since 1945*, 136-37.

Find out more

Books

1960s and 1970s (Children in History), Kate Jackson Bedford
(Franklin Watts Ltd, 2011)

Black History Makers: Musicians, Debbie Foy (Wayland, 2011)

Feminism: Ideas of the Modern World, Kaye Stearman (Raintree, 2004)

I Can Remember the 1960s, Sally Hewitt (Franklin Watts Ltd, 2010)

I Can Remember the 1970s, Sally Hewitt (Franklin Watts Ltd, 2010)

*Yeah! Yeah! Yeah!: The Beatles, Beatlemania, and the Music
That Changed the World*, Bob Spitz (Little, Brown, 2007)

Websites

kclibrary.lonestar.edu/decade70.html
Read more about American culture in the 1970s at this site.

www.biography.com/articles/Bob-Dylan-9283052
Read more about the life and career of Bob Dylan in this article.

www.americanheritage.com/content/disco
Learn more about disco music at this site.

www.allmusic.com/explore/style/british-invasion-d379
This site has lots of information about the British Invasion.

www.60smuseum.org
Explore a virtual museum of the 1960s at this site.

www.pbs.org/wgbh/amex/vietnam/index.html
Read more about the Vietnam War at this site.

www.washingtonpost.com/wp-srv/politics/special/watergate
Learn more about the Watergate Scandal at this site.

DVDs

American Mavericks: New Hollywood Cinema 1968-1972. Sony Pictures
Home Entertainment, 2009.

The Beatles Anthology. EMI, 2003.

Inside the Vietnam War. National Geographic, 2008.

Look at Life: Swinging London. Simply Media, 2010.

The Sixties: The Years That Shaped a Generation. PBS Paramount, 2005.

Those Were the Days: Britain in the Sixties. Prism Leisure Corporation, 2004.

Other resources

The Beatles Story Albert Dock
Britannia Vaults
Albert Dock
Liverpool L3 4AD

The Bill Douglas Centre for the History of Cinema and Pop Culture
The Old Library
The University of Exeter
Prince of Wales Road
Exeter
Devon EX4 4SB

Topics for further research

In 1969, some gay men in New York clashed with police at what was called the Stonewall Rebellion. The event led gays and lesbians in the United States and elsewhere to more actively assert their rights. After this, which people and events in pop culture helped to make gays more accepted by the culture at large?

Long before the Twiggy Barbie doll and Star Wars toys, popular TV shows and films had toys and games connected to them. What are some other examples of 1960s and 1970s pop culture that were turned into goods for children?

History books note the most important TV programmes of the 1960s and 1970s and their role in shaping pop culture. But bad programmes also reflect their era. Find a website or a book that describes some of the TV programmes that tried to connect with the values of the times but failed to win viewers. Why do you think the shows might not have been popular?

Choose one of the people mentioned in the book. Research more about his or her life to learn if they continued to influence their field after the 1970s.

Glossary

allies friends or supporters, especially during wartime

amplitude modulation (AM) process for sending radio signals that increases and decreases the size of the radio wave

androgynous having qualities of both a man and a woman

civil rights political freedoms, especially ones protected by the US Constitution

Cold War tense stand-off between democratic countries such as the United States and the United Kingdom, and the communist nations led by the Soviet Union. The Cold War began in 1946 (shortly after the end of World War II) and ended with the fall of the Soviet Union in 1991.

commercial referring to business or activities done to try to make money

communist referring to a political system that calls for the government to own most property and which sharply limits personal freedom

conservative tending to resist extreme changes in society or government; in politics, a person who wants a limited role for the government in the economy and supports traditional values

counterculture system of beliefs and values that is opposed to the beliefs and values of the mainstream

disc jockeys people who play records on the radio or at dance clubs

economy total goods and services produced in a given area, such as a nation or city

embroidery way of making designs on clothing using needle and thread

episode one installment of a TV or radio programme that is broadcast on a regular basis

feminism belief that men and women should have complete social, economic, and political equality

frequency modulation (FM) process for sending radio signals that increases and decreases how many radio waves are sent in a given period

fringe stringy piece of fabric that hangs off clothing

genre category of art with a particular style or subject

gospel form of emotional religious music created by African American Christians

homophobic having a strong fear or dislike of gays and lesbians

impeachment political process used to remove certain government officials from office after they do something wrong

liberal tending to be open to change or new ways of doing things; in politics, a person who favours using the power of the government to solve social problems

medium method of transmitting words or images, such as a newspaper, TV, or radio

New Age referring to a spiritual or religious view of the world that can combine elements from many religions, especially ancient ones or faiths from Asia, or accept such ideas as astrology and speaking to spirits

nuclear referring to the nucleus, or core, of tiny bits of matter called atoms; the splitting of these atoms produces huge amounts of energy that can be used in weapons

permissive allowing people to do almost anything they want, especially with regard to sex

pop art art movement based on popular culture and media. Pop artists often use found or mass-produced objects and use their work to comment on traditional art values.

radiation form of energy that can be harmful in large doses

radical extreme, compared to what most people in a society think or do

record charts lists of the most popular records, based on their sales

satellite object in space, often made by humans, that moves around other, larger objects

segregation separation of people into separate groups based on their race

sequel second or other subsequent book or film that has the same characters as the original

sitcom situation comedy, a programme that features a small cast of people dealing with a problem and solving it in a single show

soap opera programme that looks at the lives of many characters, with several stories being continued over many episodes

supermodel fashion model who becomes well known, apart from the particular clothes she wears

surreal dreamlike quality, or something that seems like reality but is somehow distorted

unisex worn or used by both men and women

value basic belief or action that defines a person's or a group's behaviour

Western referring to nations of Europe and areas where Europeans settled, which have freely elected governments and economies based on private ownership of most property

Index